DAVID COPPERFIELD

A GRAPHIC CLASSIC BY
TRINA ROBBINS

BASED ON THE NOVEL BY
CHARLES DICKENS

SCHOLASTIC INC.

New York   Toronto   London   Auckland   Sydney
Mexico City   New Delhi   Hong Kong

PENCILLER
CHARLES FRAZIER

INKER
DAVID MOWRY

COLORIST
J. BROWN AND TECH FX

LETTERER
FRED VAN LENTE

COVER ARTIST
MICHAEL LILLY

COVER COLORS
J. BROWN AND TECH FX

DAVID COPPERFIELD

WHEN CHARLES DICKENS WAS 11 YEARS OLD, HIS WHOLE FAMILY WAS PUT IN JAIL.

IT WAS THE EARLY 1800s IN ENGLAND. CHARLES'S FATHER WAS IN DEBT. AND IN THOSE DAYS, PEOPLE WHO OWED LARGE AMOUNTS OF MONEY COULD BE SENT TO PRISON. WHAT'S MORE, A DEBTOR'S FAMILY USUALLY WENT INTO PRISON, TOO.

WHEN MR. DICKENS WAS IMPRISONED, HIS WIFE AND SEVEN OF HIS CHILDREN MOVED IN WITH HIM. ONLY CHARLES STAYED BEHIND, TO WORK AT A FACTORY, EARNING MONEY FOR THE FAMILY.

THE DICKENS FAMILY WAS EVENTUALLY RELEASED, AND CHARLES WAS SENT BACK TO SCHOOL. BUT THIS STORY, AND OTHERS FROM HIS OWN LIFE, INSPIRED THE NOVEL DAVID COPPERFIELD.

MR. MURDSTONE WAS VERY STRICT WITH ME.

What is the sum of 539 plus 976?

Please, sir, I can't think when you and Miss Murdstone stare at me like that.

The boy is sullen.

Oh, Davy, do try.

If you will not *learn* your lesson, then you must be *taught* a lesson.

Oh please, no!

Davy, Davy!

Clara, you must be firm.

I WAS LOCKED IN MY ROOM.

Psst, Master Davy! It's me, Peggotty!

Peggotty!

AS SOON AS I ARRIVED AT SCHOOL, I WROTE TO PEGGOTTY.

Dear Peggotty,
I have come here safe.
Barkis is willing.
Love to mama.
Yours, DAVY

MR. CREAKLE, THE HEADMASTER, FRIGHTENED ME....

So this is young David. I know your stepfather, so I know all about you. Do you know about me?

No, sir.

You will, young man, you will!

BUT I SOON MADE FRIENDS WITH THE OTHER BOYS.

Don't worry, young Copperfield, I'll protect you.

That old Creakle doesn't scare me!

MY ONLY FRIEND DURING THAT TIME WAS PEGGOTTY, AND I SPENT MANY HOURS WITH HER IN THE KITCHEN.

Peggotty, what did Mr.Barkis mean when he said, "Barkis is willing"?

Ha ha! That old fool wants to marry me! But don't worry, Master Davy. I'll never leave you.

WHEN VACATION ENDED, I WAS NOT SORRY TO LEAVE THE MURDSTONES, BUT I WAS WORRIED ABOUT MY MOTHER AND MY NEW BROTHER. THEY SEEMED SO THIN AND PALE.

Oh Davy dear, I fear I will never see you again!

Clara, control yourself!

I HAD BEEN BACK IN SCHOOL FOR ONLY A WEEK, WHEN ...

David, please come into my office.

David, I'm sorry to tell you this. Your mother and baby brother are both dead.

Oh, Mama! Mama!

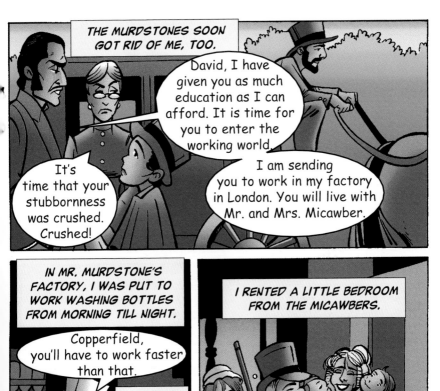

THE MURDSTONES SOON GOT RID OF ME, TOO.

David, I have given you as much education as I can afford. It is time for you to enter the working world.

It's time that your stubbornness was crushed. Crushed!

I am sending you to work in my factory in London. You will live with Mr. and Mrs. Micawber.

IN MR. MURDSTONE'S FACTORY, I WAS PUT TO WORK WASHING BOTTLES FROM MORNING TILL NIGHT.

Copperfield, you'll have to work faster than that.

I WAS ONLY TEN YEARS OLD.

I RENTED A LITTLE BEDROOM FROM THE MICAWBERS.

Copperfield, my boy, allow me to introduce Emma, my angel, my life— in short, my wife.

Ah, dear boy, I never thought I should have to take in a lodger. But Mr. Micawber's difficulties are almost overwhelming at present.

13

MR. MICAWBER OWED MONEY TO EVERYONE. HIS CREDITORS WOULD SHOW UP AS EARLY AS SEVEN O'CLOCK IN THE MORNING.

Go away! He isn't here!

We know it's you! Pay us, will you?

You just pay us, do you hear?

THE SITUATION GREW WORSE....

David, I must inform you that, except for a piece of cheese, there is not a scrap of food in the kitchen. In short, there is nothing to eat.

I have some money ...

Ah, no! But I still have some silver left.

If you would be so kind ... In short, if you would pawn this for me ...

MR. MICAWBER'S DEBTS CAUGHT UP WITH HIM, AND HE WAS SENT TO PRISON.

Are you all moving into prison?

Certainly! He is the parent of my children. He is the father of my twins. He is the husband of my affections. In short, I will never desert Mr. Micawber!

AUNT BETSEY HAD HER SERVANT THROW ME INTO A BATHTUB.

Now close your eyes, or you'll get soap in them.

THEN AUNT BETSEY FED ME.

Mmmm! Tha's goom!

Don't talk with your mouth full, boy.

THEN SHE PUT ME TO BED.

Poor fellow.

NEXT MORNING ...

I have written to your stepfather and told him you are here.

Oh, please don't send me back to Mr. Murdstone, Aunt Betsey!

AND THE NEXT DAY ...

Donkeys on my lawn! I hate donkeys!

Well! Such manners!

How dare you? You are trespassing on my land! Off with you!

Aunt Betsey, it's the Murdstones!

Miss Trotwood, that boy ran away from his job and made himself into a common tramp. He has a sullen spirit and a violent temper.

Of all the boys in the world, I believe that he is the worst boy.

Really? You don't say?

But I am ready to take him back and deal with him properly.

And what do you say, David?

Please don't make me go with them, Aunt Betsey!

They made Mama unhappy, and they made me miserable, too.

I know what kind of life you must have made for this poor child and his mother!

You broke his mother's heart and sent her to an early grave. I'll take my chances with the boy.

Well! I must say!

And if I catch you riding a donkey on my lawn again, I'll knock your bonnet off and stamp on it!

The nerve!

Oh, thank you, Aunt Betsey!

Nonsense! Now what shall I do with you? You'll need some clothes.

And I think I'll give you a new name—Trotwood Copperfield.

THANKFULLY, SHE SOON SHORTENED THAT TO TROT.

THUS I BEGAN MY NEW LIFE WITH A NEW NAME.

I'm sending you to a good school in Canterbury, Trot. You'll stay with my lawyer, Mr. Wickfield.

I trust him with my money, and I shall trust him with you, too.

I hope you'll be happy here, young man. This is Agnes, my only daughter. She runs my house for me.

I LIKED THE WICKFIELDS IMMEDIATELY.

I VISITED AGNES IN CANTERBURY, TO TELL HER ALL ABOUT IT.

Oh Agnes, I'm in love with the most beautiful girl in the world, and her name is Dora!

I ... I'm very happy for you, Trot.

AND I WENT TO MR. WICKFIELD'S OFFICE....

Heep!

I'm Mr. Wickfield's partner now, but I'm just as 'umble as before. And I have a new assistant, who I believe is a friend of yours.

Micawber!

My dear Copperfield, the companion of my youth!

Of my friend Heep, I speak with all possible respect. I am now devoted to my friend Heep's service.

In short, he got me out of debt.

What a reward to be so trusted by Mr. Wickfield and the beautiful Agnes. I wish you good-day, Master Copperfield, and send my 'umble respects to your aunt.

HEEP'S HAND WAS STILL COLD AND CLAMMY. I HATED HIM.

HEEP INSISTED ON SEEING ME OUT.

May I confide in you, Master Copperfield? Now that I'm Wickfield's partner, I hope to make Agnes my wife.

You what?!?

You swine! Agnes Wickfield is as far above you as the moon!

OW!!!

MY DEAR DORA WAS NOT STRONG, AND SHE GOT SERIOUSLY ILL.

When I can run about again, as I used to, Doady, I shall make Jip race. He's getting slow and lazy.

The doctor says it will be just a few days more, my dear.

BUT I WAS MORE WORRIED THAN I ADMITTED.

ONE DAY I RECEIVED A LETTER.

It's from Mr. Micawber, Aunt Betsey!

He asks us both to come to Mr. Wickfield's office immediately. He says it's very important.

You go, Trot. I don't want to leave Dora.

Peggotty can take care of me. I will never forgive you if you make your poor aunt stay behind.

Anyway, why shouldn't you both go? I'm not seriously ill, am I?

What a question! Of course not!

WHEN WE ARRIVED AT CANTERBURY ...

URIAH HEEP

Ssh! You are about to witness an announcement of an important nature. In short, a surprise.

Announcing Miss Trotwood, Mr. David Copperfield, Mr. Wickfield, and Miss Wickfield!

URIAH HEEP

Well! If I may 'umbly express myself, this is an unexpected pleasure.

You may go, Micawber.

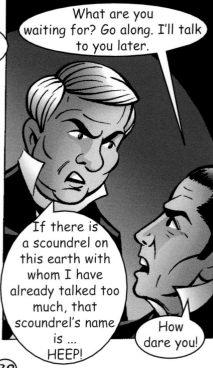

What are you waiting for? Go along. I'll talk to you later.

If there is a scoundrel on this earth with whom I have already talked too much, that scoundrel's name is ... HEEP!

How dare you!

I RETURNED HOME TO MY DEAREST DORA.

When I can run about again as I used to, Doady, let's take walks to the places we used to go.

Yes we will, and we'll be very happy. So you must hurry and get well, my dear.

Oh, I'll do that! I'm already so much better!

BUT NOW I KNEW DORA WOULD NOT GET BETTER.

Doady dear, don't think me silly, but I'm afraid I was too young to be a good wife.

We have been very happy, my sweet Dora.

Now I want to speak to Agnes alone. When you go downstairs, send her up to me.

AGNES WROTE TO ME WHILE I WAS TRAVELING.

Monsieur Copperfield? This mail arrived for you last week.

READING HER LETTERS, I SUDDENLY REALIZED ...

Agnes! What a fool I've been! I've always loved Agnes!

IMMEDIATELY I BOOKED PASSAGE BACK TO ENGLAND.

She's probably in love with someone else by now, and it's my fault. I threw away my chance with her long ago.